THE INDIANAPOLIS COLTS

Sloan MacRae

PowerKiDS
press.

New York

Published in 2011 by The Rosen Publishing Group, Inc.
29 East 21st Street, New York, NY 10010

First Edition

Editor: Amelie von Zumbusch
Book Design: Greg Tucker
Layout Design: Julio Gil

Photo Credits: Cover (Peyton Manning), pp. 5, 21, 22 (middle) Andy Lyons/Getty Images; cover (Marshall Faulk), p. 17 Rick Stewart/Getty Images; cover (Johnny Unitas), pp. 11, 13, 22 (top) Walter Iooss Jr./Sports Illustrated/Getty Images; cover (background), p. 9 Joe Robbins/Getty Images; p. 7 Al Tielemans/Sports Illustrated/Getty Images; p. 15 Ronald C. Modra/Sports Imagery/Getty Images; p. 19 Stephen Dunn/Getty Images; p. 22 (bottom) Eliot J. Schechter/Getty Images.

Library of Congress Cataloging-in-Publication Data

MacRae, Sloan.
  The Indianapolis Colts / by Sloan MacRae. — 1st ed.
      p. cm. — (America's greatest teams)
  Includes index.
  ISBN 978-1-4488-2577-6 (library binding) — ISBN 978-1-4488-2743-5 (pbk.) —
ISBN 978-1-4488-2744-2 (6-pack)
  1. Indianapolis Colts (Football team)—History—Juvenile literature. 2. Baltimore Colts (Football team)—History—Juvenile literature. I. Title.
  GV956.I53M34 2011
  796.332'640977252—dc22
                                    2010034365

Manufactured in the United States of America

CPSIA Compliance Information: Batch #WW11PK: For Further Information contact Rosen Publishing, New York, New York at 1-800-237-9932

CONTENTS

AFRAID OF THE COLTS

The Indianapolis Colts are now one of the most successful teams in football. This was not always the case. The Colts have played through some hard times. Other teams might have given up, but the Colts held on. The Colts have picked great players and **coaches** over the years. In fact, many football fans believe that the two greatest **quarterbacks** in football history have played for the Colts.

Today, Indianapolis, Indiana, has one of the most feared teams in the National Football **League**, or the NFL. None of the other NFL teams ever look forward to playing the Colts.

Today, Peyton Manning plays quarterback for the Colts. He is considered one of the best quarterbacks of all time.

HORSESHOE HEADS

The Colts used to be based in Baltimore, Maryland. Baltimore is known for horse racing. This is why the team is named the Colts. Colts are young horses. It is a good name for the team because the Colts are known for having a very fast **offense**.

Every NFL team has a special sign called a **logo**. The Colts logo is a horseshoe. This logo is on the side of the Colts' **helmets**. Fans joke that the logo makes the players look like they have been kicked in the heads by horses. Some people call the Colts Horseshoe Heads.

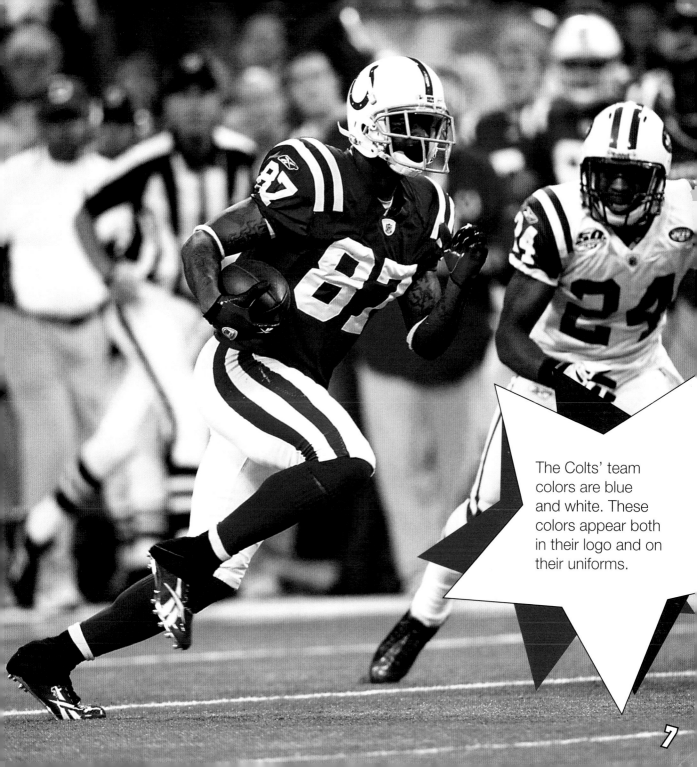

The Colts' team colors are blue and white. These colors appear both in their logo and on their uniforms.

LOUD AND PROUD

The Colts play in Lucas Oil **Stadium,** in Indianapolis. This stadium has a roof that slides in and out. The roof lets the Colts play either indoors or outdoors.

The Colts always have a great **home-field advantage** because the fans at Lucas Oil Stadium are so loud. They are loudest when the roof is closed. The noise helps the Colts because it can throw the other team off. Other NFL teams hate playing in Lucas Oil Stadium.

The Colts might play in Indianapolis, but they have fans all across the nation. They are one of the most **popular** teams in the NFL.

Here is Lucas Oil Stadium full of fans at a 2009 Colts game. The Colts played their first game in the stadium in 2008.

BALTIMORE COLTS

There have been two **professional** football teams called the Baltimore Colts. The first was formed in 1947. Baltimore sports fans loved having a professional football team in their city. The Colts did not play well, though. They struggled and went out of business in 1951.

The team's fans were mad. They wanted a new Colts team. That team formed in 1953. It quickly became one of the best teams in the NFL. The new Colts won two NFL **championships** in the 1950s. There was no such thing as the **Super Bowl** yet. The winner of an NFL championship was the top team in the NFL.

Lenny Moore, seen here, joined the Colts in 1956. He would go on to become a big star for the team.

JOHNNY UNITAS

A quarterback named Johnny Unitas joined the Colts in 1956. He stayed with the team through the 1972 season. Today many football fans believe he was the greatest quarterback ever. He was so good at throwing passes that he was nicknamed the Golden Arm. Unitas and the Colts claimed two NFL championships during the 1950s.

The 1958 Championship Game is still called the Greatest Game Ever Played. Unitas led the Colts against the New York Giants in a very close game. The Colts won, and the NFL gained many fans across the nation. This one game made football a top American sport.

Unitas (center) set many records. Between 1957 and 1960, he threw passes that led to touchdowns for a record-breaking 47 games in a row.

THE MOVE TO INDIANAPOLIS

The Colts were a great team for many years. They struggled in the mid-1970s and 1980s, though. Fewer fans bought tickets to games. It became harder to keep a professional football team in Baltimore. The Colts wanted a new stadium. The city leaders disagreed about how to raise enough money to build it.

In 1984, the Colts moved to Indianapolis. Baltimore football fans were crushed. In 1996, Baltimore finally got a new NFL team, called the Baltimore Ravens. Today Ravens fans are still angry about the Colts' move. They refuse to call the team the Colts. They just call them Indianapolis.

Bert Jones (center) played quarterback for the Colts in the 1970s and early 1980s. He was named the NFL's most valuable player, or MVP, in 1976.

FOOTBALL IN INDIANA

The Colts had a new city, but they were not a better team. They played poorly for the rest of the 1980s. They reached the **play-offs** only once.

The 1990s did not begin well either. The Colts won only one game during the 1991 season. They got better over the next few seasons. They even reached the play-offs in both 1995 and 1996. They **drafted** excellent players in the 1990s, such as Marshall Faulk and Marvin Harrison. In 1998, the Colts made one of the best draft picks in the history of football. They picked a young quarterback named Peyton Manning.

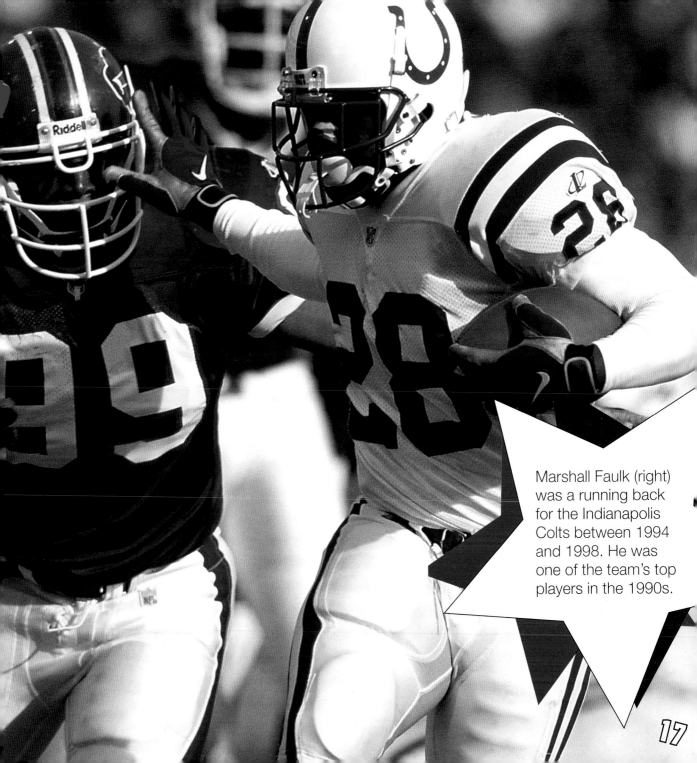

Marshall Faulk (right) was a running back for the Indianapolis Colts between 1994 and 1998. He was one of the team's top players in the 1990s.

THE RIGHT MANNING FOR THE JOB

The old Baltimore Colts had one of the greatest players of all time in Johnny Unitas. Now the Indianapolis Colts had Peyton Manning. Manning proved himself such a skilled and smart quarterback that the Colts became one of the best teams in football. They broke many NFL records.

Manning led the Colts to the play-offs nearly every season. They reached the Super Bowl in 2007 and beat the Chicago Bears. Colts head coach Tony Dungy became the first African-American head coach to win a Super Bowl. Indianapolis reached the Super Bowl again in 2010. Sadly, the Colts lost to the New Orleans Saints.

Dungy (right) and Manning (left) worked well together. The Colts reached the play-offs every season that they were both with the team.

HARD TO BEAT

In 2009, the Colts set an NFL record by winning 23 regular-season games in a row. They continue to be one of the hardest teams to beat in professional football. Their offense can score a lot of points in a very short amount of time. Great players such as Peyton Manning, Reggie Wayne, and Joseph Addai keep the Colts winning big games and breaking records.

The Colts' hard times are far behind them. The team looks forward to winning more championships for their very loud fans. The Colts remain the only team in the NFL that enjoys playing in Indianapolis.

The Colts picked running back Joseph Addai (center) in the 2006 NFL Draft. Addai had a great first year and went on to become a star for the team.

INDIANAPOLIS COLTS TIMELINE

1953

The new Baltimore Colts beat the Chicago Bears in their first game.

1956

Johnny Unitas joins the Colts.

1957

The Colts put the horseshoe logo on the sides of their helmets.

1958

The Colts beat the New York Giants in the Greatest Game Ever Played.

1984

The Colts move to Indianapolis.

1998

The Colts pick Peyton Manning in the NFL draft.

2002

Tony Dungy becomes the Colts' head coach.

2007

The Colts beat the Chicago Bears in the Super Bowl.

2009

The Colts beat the Jacksonville Jaguars and set an NFL record with 23 regular-season wins in a row.

GLOSSARY

CHAMPIONSHIPS (CHAM-pee-un-ships) Official names of the best or the winner.

COACHES (KOHCH-ez) People who direct teams.

DRAFTED (DRAFT-ed) Picked to play on a professional sports team.

HELMETS (HEL-mits) Coverings worn to keep the head safe.

HOME-FIELD ADVANTAGE (hohm-FEELD ad-VAN-tij) The edge teams get when they play in their own stadium.

LEAGUE (LEEG) A group of sports teams.

LOGO (LOH-goh) A picture, words, or letters that stand for a team or company.

OFFENSE (O-fents) When a team tries to score points in a game.

PLAY-OFFS (PLAY-ofs) Games played after the regular season ends to see who will play in the championship game.

POPULAR (PAH-pyuh-lur) Liked by lots of people.

PROFESSIONAL (pruh-FESH-nul) Having players who are paid.

QUARTERBACKS (KWAHR-ter-baks) Football players who direct their teams' plays.

STADIUM (STAY-dee-um) A place where sports are played.

SUPER BOWL (SOO-per BOHL) The championship game of NFL football.

INDEX

WEB SITES

Due to the changing nature of Internet links, PowerKids Press has developed an online list of Web sites related to the subject of this book. This site is updated regularly. Please use this link to access the list:
www.powerkidslinks.com/teams/fcolts/